face your self.

look within.

xo. adrian michael

THOUGHT
CATALOG
Books

THOUGHTCATALOG.COM

**THOUGHT
CATALOG
Books**

Published by Thought Catalog Books, an imprint of Thought Catalog, a digital magazine owned and operated by The Thought & Expression Co. Inc., an independent media organization founded in 2010 and based in the United States of America. For stocking inquiries, contact stockists@shopcatalog.com.

Produced by Chris Lavergne and Noelle Beams
Art direction and design by KJ Parish
Creative editorial direction by Brianna Wiest
Circulation management by Isidoros Karamitopoulos

thoughtcatalog.com | shopcatalog.com

First Edition, Limited Edition Pressing
Printed in the United States of America.

ISBN 978-1-949759-74-7

the greatest love comes from you.
the kind of love you let grow wild.
the kind of love you water from
your deep soul. thank you for
giving even when the same
depth never is returned.
xo. adrian michael

for all who
dare to face
themselves.

a playlist*

please don't go x tank
breaking point x leon thomas
find you x maths time joy
slowly x jon vinyl
amazing x teddy swims
stay x goapele + bj the chicago kid
you x yellow days
misunderstood x lucky daye
love like that x snoh aalegra
warm embrace x chris brown
exhausted x h.e.r.
some unspoken thing x leuca
love jones x leon thomas + ty dolla $ign
take it slow x dvsn
notice me x sza
violet x daniel caesar
us x fkj
learn ya x 6lack
obsession x eric bellinger + muni long
more than love x trevor hall
all up in your mind x beyoncé
never seen the rain x tones and i
monster x shawn mendes + justin bieber
breathe x seinabo sey
time x giveon
gotta move on x diddy + bryson tiller

incense. palo santo. candles. sage.
tea. whiskey. wine. water. beer.

*to be listened to. lit and sipped while reading or
between readings for ultimate experience.
search "face yourself. look within." on itunes or spotify
to stream the playlist that is waiting for you.

six agreements**

use to build trust and commitment. use to anchor you. use to focus you. use to remind you. use to find your way home.

be fully present. when you are doing this work be with this work. turn off distractions. when your attention goes away acknowledge its going and come back. come back.

lean into discomfort. if some concepts and language herein triggers you tells you close this go away from this stay this. stand in the fire a bit longer. this isn't an overnight read. let growth happen slowly.

host the journey. share this when it feels good to. with those close. with those you trust. to wonder together. to learn together. to push together. you not as expert. but you as light)one of the lights(to inspire healing magic to make better. to love better. to be better.

give you what you need. some of this may not land with you. some of this may not be a one-to-one. make it relevant to you. seek the lesson. translate it in ways that make sense to where you are in life.

honor your process. in moments of confidence and confidentiality you can keep you to you. keep this to you. never feel like you have to announce your story your journey your wondering. make sure that along the way you celebrate how far you have come.

practice. this isn't meant to just stay stagnant. this is meant to be breathed out and in. out and in. for yourself. for the world. to try out. to try on. to probe and fill holes and connect bridges and break down barriers. to deeper connect by seeing you in the mirror and the humanity of others you may not have seen before)really really seen(. so be willing to get messy. be raggedy. not perfect)never perfect(. to make room for you. to make room for others. you decide what this looks like feels like sounds like in practice. in real time. to learn and unlearn. learn and unlearn.

*to take with you on this journey. try them. scrap them. write your own. peace be unto you. **copyright lovasté adapted by agreements encouraged by nais and the national equity project.

words for you

trust your heart more often.

if you're not feeling it then don't do it.
trust what your heart tells you more often.

focus. center. breathe. peace.

focus. on what you can control. no use in placing all your energy towards what's out of your hands. instead of worrying about what if focus on what can. what can you do. what can you try. what can you tend to. that kind of focus. focus. focus.

center. your thoughts. your heart. your body. and find stability when feeling shaky. to ground you. to hold you. to balance you. to help bring clarity in chaos. go inside whirlwinds and create quietness. create calm. allow fast pace to become slow. slow. slow. seek your center. center. center.

breathe. close your eyes and look for the movement you create in and around you. consider what all you allow in your orbit and what isn't serving your life. inhale deeper now. release. the air of you is sacred. the air in you is sacred. breathe. breathe. breathe.

peace. a state of being even when all around you is tumultuous and unkind. you bring serenity. you are serenity. you are stillness and monumental. no need to add strain. be peace. feel peace. request peace. peacefulness is grace that fills the soul.

focus yourself.
center yourself.
breathe yourself.
peace yourself.

six nudges to keep you on the right path.

use your influence for good.
do what you can to help others.
you don't have all the answers.
your heart is in the right place.
criticism is to be expected.
do it anyway.

for when you don't know what you need.

you don't always have to know what you need. your response may not be perfect or articulate the way someone else can understand but you're doing the best you can by trying. the root of something isn't clear until you dig. so dig at your time. at your choosing. but don't take your frustration out on those closest to you. don't take your frustrations out on anyone.

if you don't know what's going on with you say you need grace.

say you need space to process.
say you need space to breathe.
say you need space to piece.
say you need space to be.
it's okay to request space.
it's okay to take space.

and even in that space you take you may not find anything.

sometimes the answer is the pause.
sometimes the answer is the break.
sometimes the answer is the space.

***

what you're experiencing doesn't require understanding. it requires active listening. active hearing. active holding. active loving. you don't have to make sense or prove your pain or sorrow or hide your joy or smile. all of you is accepted. you need to know this beloved.

words to tell yourself.

thank you for seeing me. when i feel unseen.
thank you for loving me. when i feel unloved.
thank you for wanting me. when i feel unwanted.
thank you for hearing me. when i feel unheard.

tell this to you.
tell this to others.

how to be okay being misunderstood.

everyone won't see the world how you see the world.
everyone won't value what you value. it isn't on you
to translate the steps you take to anyone.

it's on you to evaluate each step. appreciate each step.
question each step. that you choose to take. narrating
your life is up to you.

you will always be misunderstood by those chasing answers
they haven't resolved for themselves. this is your advantage.
this is your power. this is your calling. to vision what no one else
visions. such magic is misunderstood love and light.

you're left to turn into whatever it is you want to turn into.
that is your meant to. that is your mission. no need to
seek validation.

there is beauty in your wonder. no misunderstanding that.
there is beauty in your awe. no misunderstanding that.
there is beauty in you. no misunderstanding that.

***

*reaching for you is the best kind of reaching. it is you that only
gets it. that feeling. that feeling. that being outside the box.
that being outside the lines. how brave it is to create
your own instead of being confined. you're
accepted because you)you(
accept yourself.*

five ways to love better.

understand your communication style. nothing can get done without the transfer of language. verbal and non-verbal. it is never one-sided. if you are receiving an attitude from someone that offends you or doesn't align with where you are trying to go or get to maybe it is because they are just responding to yours. you can't control what they do but you can be in control of the communication you are sending. the majority of issues arise because of huge breakdowns in this area. develop in this area.

notice your listening style. do you listen to respond or do you listen to hear. truly hear. can you pick up on the nuances and meanings. do you jump to conclusions before they are done speaking. if your attention isn't on them it's better to request another time when you have the capacity and share that you want to concentrate on them but at the moment it isn't possible. this is an important skill that is too often overlooked and assumptions over what someone said creates more barriers.

follow through. the ideas are great and the intention is even greater but something stops you from complete execution. whether that is lost interest or energy or moved on to another thing but if you get good at being 70% with something then 70% will carry into the next thing and the next. so instead get good at follow-through. finish what you start. do what it is you said you were going to do. there is something to say about someone who can tap into last gear and finish the race.

make coffee. it's the little things that people remember. they will forget what you said but how you made them feel forever remains. maya angelou reminds us of that. it is so true. imagine taking the time to bring you something that you don't have to think about or exhaust yourself having to do. they bring you lunch so you don't forget to eat. they stock the fridge with your favorite treats. making coffee is about creating space for your person to focus instead of stress.

be willing to try new things. comfort zones are real. we have them for a reason. there is not much to try there. but they can also limit us from growing and experiencing more that is out there to learn and see. we all like different things and what intrigues you may not intrigue another. but doing something with someone is less about being comfortable and more about willingness to lean in and share in their joy. of course be mindful of your boundaries and values and trust that there is a love lesson there.

***

people grow in and out of love because they aren't willing to grow together. yes life happens and things don't work out and some folks just shouldn't be together. but if you are in a healthy and loving and nurturing situation or are working towards that then it is worth fighting for if there is *love* there. if there is *give* there. if there is *commitment* there. love looks different but at its core you should feel like you're safe and whole.

grow together or depart from one another.

four roses that make a bouquet.

thought.

    meaning.

        energy.

            love.

what you rarely hear but should always know.

*your energy is contagious. the way you do what
you do has major impact. no one else can change
the tone and tenor of a room like you can. nobody
else cares the type of care you infuse. thankful
doesn't quite hit the core as to the feelings you
make others feel just by being you. you have
every right to want to stop and break and end
and do something different but you stay and
that means everything to the ones used to
being left behind. you are amazing do you
know that? amazing amazing. grateful
for your big kind heart.*

your feelings are valid.

your feelings are valid
even if no one validates
them.

even if you don't think you're blooming you are.

on the other side of this there is you. standing.
talling. rising. and as the dust settles all that it
took to get you to where you're meant to be
will be patches adorned around you in memory
and remembrance and remind you of the times
that tried to contain you. tried to bar you. tried
to scar you. tried to deny you. tried to keep you
from the other side. times like these teach you.
equip you. test you. to golden your wings and
it doesn't feel like that now. but growth is
uncomfortable. the stretch. the resistance.
the energy. the challenge. even if you
don't think you're blooming you are.

feel the weight lift when you hear this.

it's not your fault.
you did what you could.
thanks for speaking your truth.
you didn't deserve to be carrying that.
give me all your burdens all your worries.
no you aren't bothering me tell me everything.
clearing my schedule just for you just for you.
what do you need and i got you i got you.
if you want to come home come home.
you are the definition of inspiration.
here to listen not to fix you.
you are beautiful magic.

affirmations for you.

may the old versions of you
not be used against you.
held against you. to apprehend
your new light.

may your sun look for you in dark places
so you can find your way back to you.

may what you need be felt and not just heard.

may the games people play with your heart
come to an end and only the well-intentioned
have access to your ocean and horizon.

affirmations for you. II

may you joy and joy and joy and joy and joy and joy and joy and joy and joy and joy and joy and joy and joy and joy and joy without feeling guilty or obligated to permit yourself to embrace the good in your life.

may soul kisses find you and feather you in all the spots that need finding and feathering.

may that smile)that smile(be wide and free.
full and real. you and you. today and always.
today and always.

for when you feel judged.

don't let their words distract you.
don't let their opinion stop you.
don't let their thorns pierce you.

you know your heart.
you know your why.

and if their judgments occupy your mind: you are human.
it's going to happen. you will swirl and feel attacked and
even want to defend yourself. it's not your responsibility
to convince them. you can listen and thank them for
their criticism but you don't have to take them with you.

***

sometimes people are set in what things are supposed to be like.
what things are supposed to feel like. push back against that. go
outside the lines. follow your own tune to find your lane and
create a life that ignites you. let your light be their greeting. no
use in feeding any more negative energy.

their judgment isn't about you it's about them.
send them in love. send them in love.

don't dim yourself by letting judgment in.
love yourself by recognizing the difference
between healthy feedback and
harmful scrutiny.

the best kind of friend.

the best kind of friend catapults you. rocks for you.
roots for you. shouts for you. even if in their own
life it feels like nothing is going right for them.
friendship is about being able to say *right on*
let's celebrate you but damn i'm having a
rough go and knowing one of us is on
top is beautiful goodness soon to
rub off during a season on the
horizon but it won't stop me
from riding tough for you.
best friends are an
eternal love.

***

may the friendships you have
keep you level. keep you afloat.
keep you watered as you water
them. nothing better than a
solid friend that ships you
what you need before
it is needed. shows
up one hour even if it takes
longer just to get to you.
supports you and doesn't bash
you when your lives moves
your waters in different directions.
hold on to friends like this. always.

how to be a good friend.

be unselfish. how can i support you.
be open. how i can hold you.
be flexible. how long can i stay.

good friends fill voids just by stepping into the friendship with
the desire to care. desire to witness. desire to love. it's more than
pleasantries and good news and keeping up with pretenses. it's
the taking off the mask and getting soul level. being rock and
water. when you have a circle of friends like this)like antidote
and air(stay around them.

good friends are like antidote and air.
good friends are like antidote and air.
good friends are like antidote and air.
good friends are like antidote and air.
good friends are like antidote and air.

***

good friends are hard to come by.
some are seasonal. some are forever.
some are mixed with something special.
the best ones grab you by heart and
allow you to be you even when
you feel some kind of way
about being you.

stay close to friends who cherish your light.

maybe.

maybe. just maybe. what you
have been looking for was right
there)right there(in front of you.
you were just too hyperfocused
and the seeing of it was illusive
was too good was impossible
to actually be there. maybe.
just maybe. you wanted
something else. maybe.

maybe. just maybe. you don't need
what you think you need. but you
clench to it want it so badly so
muchly that that that that
needing is delaying you
keeping you longer
than you deserve
to be kept.
maybe.

maybe. just maybe. the searching.
the wandering. the processing.
is the point. is the everything.
is the is the. maybe.
just maybe.
you're closer.
you're closer.

maybe. just maybe. learning you is the breath that's been missing.

prioritize you.

for once. prioritize you. decide that right now is your time.

your space. to create for yourself what you've needed. what your heart has been swelling for. and you with an outstretched hand outstretched soul outstretched well can't keep giving. can't keep loving. can't keep watering undeserving. can't keep them on display when they have never put you up on anything. and when you pull away they will shrivel and wonder why you went where you went and how can they get more)this always happens(and sipping from your own reserve say never again.

for when enough is enough.

you are entitled to

your opinion.
your perspective.
your experience.
your currency.

you are not entitled to

explain away the story of another and tell them that what they
are seeing. what they are feeling. what they are living isn't valid.
if you meet them where they are and listen)just listen(you'll
hear different. you'll be different.

an anti-racist statement.

if anti-racism isn't part
of your learning you aren't
really learning.

anti-racism is a process. it isn't check the box. had that training. had that conference. had that issue now it's on to the next. anti-racism is an active awareness for the checking on blindspots in all the areas people and beings living and unliving are involved. it is social. political. economic. environmental. educational. everything. it isn't standalone it's intersectional. combined with and in connection to other structural institutional and individual isms that need to be examined. both and. all and. anti-racism means you are working towards equity through a racial lens that is window and mirror. a looking within. a looking without downplaying racialized experiences and perspectives you've never had to think about. it means doing the work to dismantle racist policies and practices in you.

for your heart to feel.

your ancestors are proud of you.
it's okay to stop responding to people
who only reach out when they need
something. you don't have to explain
your heart here. this version of you
is the greatest version you have
ever been. the timing of
your life isn't on any
one's schedule
but your
own.

***

that unexpected thing that rattled you.
isn't an always it is just temporary.

that unexpected thing that shook you.
isn't an always it is just temporary.

that unexpected thing that thorned you.
isn't an always it is just temporary.

glad you are here.

how to find yourself when you get lost.

you're never lost.
remember where you were.
remember where you are.
never forget where
you come from.

look around you and behold
all the beautiful things that
once were seeds and now
sprouted beyond your
wildest dreams.

if you aren't fulfilled
get to filling yourself.
no one can fill you
how you fill you.

***

you aren't lost.
you are looking.

if those around you don't see
what you see and tell you they
can't see what you see and try
to avert your eyes to other
things they understand
keep your eyes keep your eyes
and your heart)keep your heart(
on digging and finding and
you'll find yourself there.

how to find yourself when you get lost. II

give yourself the roses.
give yourself the favors.
give yourself the grace.

this life beloved is about the search.
about the rescue. about the pursuit
of you trying to keep your light
and the light of others from burning
out without taking. without depleting.
without harming and having the
courageous audacity to find why
you were one of the beautiful beings
to live. so live and lead with love.

four types of peace you deserve.

peace to make your own decisions.
peace to discover who you are.
peace from being discouraged.
peace from unpeaceful spaces.

it won't always be calm but it shouldn't always be toxic.
you can't grow around energy that blocks your sunlight
constantly. that type of setting is exhausting. sometimes
it is worth it to travel uphill but not with people trying to
pull you down. pull away from their chaos.

you're not as expected. you're better.

you're not as expected. you're better.
you're not as dreamed. you're better.
you're not as imagined. you're better.
you're not as needed. you're better.

better love. that's you love. full love.
hear love. here love. thankful love.
for your being love. for being
beyond the scope of my
looking. peace love.
you give me peace
love. peace love.

what you deserve to know.
what you deserve to hear.
recite this. hold this.

for when you are having a hard time.

beloved. when i ask if you're okay
know that you can say you're not.
there is no need to comfort your
hardship denying its existence.
even if you say you're having
a difficult time and that's all
you want to share then i'll
respect that and be there
without another word.

28 lessons.

trust. boundary. reflect. decide. leap. slow.
space. rest. remember. stretch. water. be.
face. do. open. awaken. peace. depart.
imagine. play. laugh. mistake. miss.
devote. unfold. balance. stay. love.

empty empty.

you can hear the words over and over from people. the kind of words you want to hear. need to hear. deserve to hear. but if it doesn't come from that person)your person(that one you really need to feel it from, it just doesn't land the same. it's empty. empty. empty.

your heart says:
a refill from you is the perfect end to a hard day.
how is it that you know what to do.
how is it that you know what to say.
how is it that you know what to bring.
how is it that you know what to fill.

you provide this fullness to others.
you provide this fullness in others.

so even as you think what is from you
doesn't matter or make a difference it does.

anything else is just off brand. off you.
don't allow anyone who tries to duplicate
you dim your light love. love from you
is the best light love.

you person says:
i only want your light love.
i only want your love love.
no one can fill how you
fill love. no one. no
one. no one.

the little things.

it may seem like the little things
you're doing now won't amount to anything.
the waking. the breathing. the timing. the
waiting. the training. the pausing. the
leading. the commuting. the studying. the
planning. the shedding. the leaving. the
crying. the resting. the giving. the
caring. the creating. the loving. the
loving. the loving. it is in these
little things)always the little things(
that grow into every things. these
are the details that matter love.

abundance is coming.

this season can feel like you are losing but in fact you are shedding. what isn't for you is leaving you. taking another route. not to get to you. it's during low tides when you can be preparing. tinkering. attempting. see this time as playful opportunity. not for getting down on yourself. abundance is coming. this season you can hibernate. don't feel forced to create. abundance is coming. this season you can tend to nothing. you can choose not to do anything. abundance is coming. this season you are growing even though you may not see it. everything around you changes. everything around you feels you. abundance is coming. this season is yours to season. yours to decide what accesses you and what doesn't clear what used to come and go but now can't find you. abundance is coming. this season is _____.
and that is beautiful and terrifying. abundance is coming. and that is easier said than done. this season)your season(may not be what you expected. may not be like the picture in your heart. in your head. in your plan. but it is something more. maybe it is something more. abundance is coming. this isn't about toxic positivity or looking at the bright side. this is about looking from the lesson love. look for the lesson love. look. for. the. lesson. love.

be someone's someone.

someone that understands your hopes.
someone that recognizes your light.
someone that waters your heart.
someone that fills your bucket.

33 lessons.

accept. let go. forgive. reflect. unlearn. respond.
speak. listen. complete. intend. attend. notice.
practice. love. apologize. change. empathize.
lean in. prioritize. courage. accountability.
gratitude. joy. manifest. patience.
commitment. presence. grace.
understanding. consider.
believe. breathe.
give.

how to speak their heart language.

be yourself. show up as the person you are.
be consistent. show you can be relied upon.
be vulnerable. share your knowledge.
be careful. protect what they present to you and only you.
be loyal. at the sign of a storm don't retreat. run towards
them while it rains and thunders. **be mirror**. don't be
their answer. be their sounding board. their person
to help see who they are without telling them who
they need to be. **be willing**. to grow together.
and stand in the fire together. let them in.

***

don't teach me. don't show me.
just be. just be. and i'll adore
all of your being. side by side
through it all to see our scars
as beauty marks and clues of
where we can begin again to
make amends and plant our
hearts and harvest love each
and every day. you're my every
day love. my every day love.

how to say sorry to someone you hurt.

i. *my bad. i didn't know.*
it wasn't my intention.
but that doesn't matter.
what matters is that it
impacted you. it hurt
you. i hurt you.

ii. *if i knew then what i know now*
i'd go back. i'd go back. and do it
 differently.

iii. *i should have said this sooner.*
i just didn't know what to say.
how to say. what to do. or how
you would respond. this isn't
an excuse. i'm deeply sorry.

iv. *you don't have to say anything.*
i can tell i've caused a shift. a rift.
an imbalance. it's on me to repair it.
i want to repair it. to bring us back.

the best sorry is sincere. it isn't jammed with excuses. with deflections. with gaslighting. with anything pointed at the person directly impacted by the situation. the best sorry is honest. it comes from a place of understanding that no matter the intention, the impact caused harm and that means the intent doesn't really matter. the follow up. the changed behavior is what matters. even if you think you're not at fault. let that last one simmer.

ten compassionate questions.

what's your path?
where do you want to go?
where are you headed?
who are you? who are you with?
who are you surrounded by?
who do you want to be surrounded by?
what version of you are you right now?
what version of you are you becoming?
what version are you on the edge of
breaking into blooming into?

love like this.

intentionally.
specifically.
honestly.
openly.
truthfully.
carefully.
respectfully.
willfully.
daringly.
courageously.
slowly.
gracefully.

how to lose yourself.

if you must get lost
get lost of what holds you back
get lost of bitter mistreatment
get lost of negative energy
and get busy get busy get busy
looking for what is looking for you
looking for what is missing you
looking for what calls for you
and give yourself permission
to find what you think is
unfindable. you'll find it.
you'll always find you.

if someone ghosts you.

you didn't do anything wrong.
you weren't meant for them.
you deserve someone better.
you dodged their empty love.
you aren't the problem.
you can breathe now.

you take it hard and absorb messages that go
unreturned as if you did something as if you
were the reason as if you could have done
more to fit their life. but their immaturity
was a gift. don't lose sleep over them.

***

ghosting is harmful.
ghosting is toxic.
ghosting is traumatic.

*unless you have been so badly treated and disrespected and
harmed in ways that trigger you to remove someone out of your
life with no notice. with no communication. with no sign of repair.*
ghosting shouldn't be what you do to someone.

it leaves too many open wounds. too many behaviors that follow
and offend others who did nothing to earn sour treatment. too
many wrong ideas of not enoughness and distrust in others
grows stronger and the walls go up making it harder for anyone
to love them again.

everyone has their reasons. don't be that person if you don't
have to.

take what you need.

this is the one you were supposed to open to. the one meant to
lift you. the one on time when all else has felt delayed. the one
with salve. the one. the one. the one. the what you closed your
eyes for so tight the night then and the night last. and the night
now. fast with this. vibe with this. take what you need:

i. you can't be everywhere at once.
all you can be is somewhere once.
at a time. so wherever you are.
wherever you need to be. be.
be there. there there. not
partially there. fully.
there. notice how it
feels to tend to one
heart at a time.

ii. every day seems the same.
a bit lacking. a bit voiding.
a bit maddening. a bit _____.
but you get the chance to change
the channel. the weather. the
station. do something
radical today. push
yourself to find what
you stopped looking for.

iii. no longer avoid hardships.
no longer avoid sadness.
no longer avoid breakups.

take what you need. II

this is the one you were supposed to open to. the one meant to lift you. the one on time when all else has felt delayed. the one with salve. the one. the one. the one. the what you closed your eyes for so tight the night then and the night last. and the night now. fast with this. vibe with this. take what you need:

iv. just because it's easy doesn't mean it's for you. and just because it's hard doesn't mean it's meant to hurt you. there is a point you know you're accustomed to. that thin line between meaningful and toxic.

v. the lane you are creating is getting more spacious.

vi. what you are doing
was already written.
already bound.
already etched. you
just have to keep
the torch lit so
you can see
yourself
shine.

for when things don't go your way.

it may seem like nothing is going your way. and the pressure is not letting up. and no matter what you try there is no give there is no difference there is no relief just more stress. more frustration. more hesitation. more pull towards giving up. towards stopping. towards not trying anymore. and you can. you can go another way. but this way)this way(you are facing is where you want to go. where you want to be. so don't be deterred. don't be re-routed. face ahead and keep your heart open. stay in it. stay in this. you're one breath away closer. don't give up.

don't give up. you're one breath away.
don't give up. you're two breaths away.
don't give up. you're three breaths away.
don't give up. you're four breaths away.
don't give up. you're five breaths away.
don't give up. you're six breaths away.
don't give up. you're seven breaths away.
don't give up. you're eight breaths away.
don't give up. you're nine breaths away.
don't give up. you're ten breaths away.
don't give up. you're eleven breaths away.
don't give up. you're twelve breaths away.

but if you turn back. it's okay to turn back.
let there be no hard feelings. let there be
only *i did the best i could*. let there be
only *i gave my all my all my all*. let there
be only words that honor your effort.
you did. you did. you did. many
don't. many don't. many don't.

don't give up is full love.

it says:

rooting for you. cheering for you.
even if you don't notice. even if
you don't see me in your corner.
i am present. in your choices.
i am present. in your process.
i am present. in your doubts.
whatever you do i trust you.
whatever you do i back you.
whatever you do i got you.
whatever you do i rock you.
whatever you do i awe you.
whatever you do i love you.

don't give up beloved.

how to announce your rest.

thank you for your patience.

and let that be that. just say that.
no drawn out explanation. no
receipt to prove your way
was justified. no reason
you have to give other
people an excuse
for choosing
rest and
you.

you've logged all the hours to know when you need a break.
when you need to walk away. when you need to change
the scenery. the resistance to rest is that there's this
belief that you haven't earned it. that you can
only access it when someone approves it.
even in your resting they still want
access to you.

don't burn yourself out. rest.
don't think you can't. rest.
don't ask for permission. rest.
don't deny your energy. rest.
don't forget to breathe. rest.
don't think it isn't for you. rest.
don't miss your own signs. rest.
don't become their culture. rest.
don't announce your rest. rest.

rest is the greatest most underutilized way to heal yourself.

how to check in on your strong friends.

what's good. what's new. what's it been like being in your shoes in
your world lately. how'd that last project go. i know it took a lot
out of you. tap in when you get a second. not now)it doesn't have
to be now(whenever you can come up for air. you've been on my
mind. hit me back. tell the family i said hello. peace. xo.

***

such a myth that strong people don't need help from anyone.
such a myth that strong people don't need love from anyone.

the ones who do the checking.
the ones who do the giving.
the ones who do the holding.
the ones who do the everything.
they need topping up, too.
they need appreciation, too.
they need deep breaths, too.

it may look
it may feel
it may seem
that they are
always strong
always steady
always rock
but they
might not be.

heavy is the heart
expected to be
unbothered and tough.

the strongest are the softest
of them all. speak to them
how they need to be spoken
to. in the language that pulls
them. that greets their soul
as being seen)they deserve
to know they are seen(and even if they don't respond that saw
it. they got it. they
took in your love. check in on your strong friends.

let me be your well.

if you're doing tremendous or
if you're not, you can well to me.
let me be your well.

how to say i love you without words.

i. do a 360 of all the things they do.
observe what brightens them.
look in-between the cracks
others overlook. find out
one new thing daily to
show them you're
paying attention.

ii. leave a letter for them to open
nothing in it but your heart.

iii. send them a song with the exact
moment you want them to listen.

iv. make a reservation in their name
to claim whenever they have time
to get away and take a deep breath.

v. make something. any something.
the meaning behind it will mean
more than anything you can buy.

i know i said i wouldn't say anything
and i'm not. i'm not. i'm showing you.
i'm spending more time with me
probing why it took me this long
to meet you halfway. all the way.
every day is yours now. has always
been yours. i see you now. clearly now.
thought i was in a dream but you
are real love. you are real love.

cut ties with people who thorn and scorch your relationship.

cut ties with people who thorn and scorch your relationship.
cut ties with people who thorn and scorch your relationship.
cut ties with people who thorn and scorch your relationship.
cut ties with people who thorn and scorch your relationship.
cut ties with people who thorn and scorch your relationship.
cut ties with people who thorn and scorch your relationship.
cut ties with people who thorn and scorch your relationship.
cut ties with people who thorn and scorch your relationship.
cut ties with people who thorn and scorch your relationship.
cut ties with people who thorn and scorch your relationship.
cut ties with people who thorn and scorch your relationship.
cut ties with people who thorn and scorch your relationship.
cut ties with people who thorn and scorch your relationship.
cut ties with people who thorn and scorch your relationship.
cut ties with people who thorn and scorch your relationship.
cut ties with people who thorn and scorch your relationship.
cut ties with people who thorn and scorch your relationship.
cut ties with people who thorn and scorch your relationship.
cut ties with people who thorn and scorch your relationship.
cut ties with people who thorn and scorch your relationship.
cut ties with people who thorn and scorch your relationship.
cut ties with people who thorn and scorch your relationship.
cut ties with people who thorn and scorch your relationship.
cut ties with people who thorn and scorch your relationship.
cut ties with people who thorn and scorch your relationship.
cut ties with people who thorn and scorch your relationship.
cut ties with people who thorn and scorch your relationship.
cut ties with people who thorn and scorch your relationship.
cut ties with people who thorn and scorch your relationship.
cut ties with people who thorn and scorch your relationship.
cut ties with people who thorn and scorch your relationship.
cut ties with people who thorn and scorch your relationship.

how to let go.

you let go. and you level up. you level up. that old self is old
news. you were someone else then. you are someone better now.
if they compare you they don't know you. let go by letting go.
just wait)it's hard to wait(but what you are reading for is way
way better)much better(than what you thought you had before.
you just have to see it through. if not you'll miss what has been
written for you. the decision you made had to be made. it was
what was best even if it doesn't feel like it.

***

you're doing the best you can.
you're doing better than you
think you are. drop your
shoulders and get all
that tension away
from you. letting go
of what needed gone
good riddance)good good
riddance(. you deserve better.

for when you are having a hard time. II

everyone is going through
or has gone through or will
go through something that
feels like a weight they
don't want to burden
anyone else with.

with me you are no burden.
with me you are in loving hands.

for when you are having a hard time. III

there is no answer here.
there is no cure here.
there is possibility
and hope here.
to remind
you that
whatever you
are going through
i'm here. always here.

how to heal from old wounds.

you are not tied to a timeline.
you are not required to rush.
you are permitted all the time
all the space all the grace to be
so you can process your process.

ritualize your feelings.
open your heart so light
can breathe into what
you're holding back.

you don't have to justify or share.
what you are going through isn't
for audience or judgment or for
anyone to dictate your experience.

notice. what comes up.
listen. to your energy.
speak. your truth.
find. where it hurts.
trust. your self.
lean. on your people.
seek. accessible therapy.
patient. with your healing.
let. love and light in.

here for you. in whatever that looks like. daily. weekly. nightly.
rarely. tell me. if you shut me out i'll understand. grow through
this without me if you must. just know)just deeply know(i care.
i am holding space. holding you. loving you. always loving you.
here for you during and after.

how to treat yourself.

someone will always have something to say about you. don't allow their words to be what determines your worth. someone will always try to tell you what you should do. what you should think. how you should feel. if you trust them—listen. if you don't trust them listen. what you do with what they tell you is your choice. decide for yourself.

how to treat yourself. the way you would want to be treated by anyone else. and better. treat yourself better beloved. softly instead of sharply. patiently instead of rushly. kindly instead of harshly. lovingly instead of cruelly.

break from what needs to be broken from.

swiftly. even if there is pause to decide if it must be removed. it is your free will to disconnect. and replace where you would rather be. where you need to fill better. what holds you isn't exempt from investigation. it is a crucial practice to re-evaluate the difference between what is toxic and harming you and what is healthy and nourishing you. so whenever you re-write you)you get to do that as often as you like(inventory all that is with you. all that is on you. all that occupies you. and pay close attention to how you feel. even if you can't let go of what you want to let go you can decide and reframe and exchange how you think about it. if you can let go let go. some things aren't meant to stay. some things aren't meant to journey with you into the next you. no resentment. no angst. no ill will. no negativity. just release. release. release. release. break from what needs to be broken from.

for when you feel like giving up.

stop right there. before you read further. know that wanting to
give up. wanting to call it quits. wanting to throw in the towel.
is normal. that feeling you are feeling to revert back. to go back.
to retreat. to what is known. what is easier. what is comfortable.
is the human thing we all do. but quitting is easy. regret lasts
a lifetime.

so ask yourself. if you quit.
so ask yourself. if you stop.
so ask yourself. if you left.
so ask yourself. if you stayed.

would you regret it.
would you resent it.
would you repress it.
would you resist it.

giving up is a natural response for when things don't fall into
place. for when things don't go the way you want them to. for
when things looks hopeless)some things are but all things
aren't(. you just have to know)the way you only know(if you
gave it to the last drop and you've exhausted all your moves.

the grit in you. the fight in you. the you in you.

trust in you. breathe in you.
and if you give up that's okay.
and if you give up that's okay.
giving up doesn't make you
a failure. remember that.

for when you're not being refilled.

the pour sometimes doesn't reach the cup. the point is to just fall and give and spill. the catching. the receiving. the collecting. can't be on you. can't be the water and the cup to everyone. but you can be the water and the cup for you. to taste your own loving refill.

if you aren't being refilled
the way you deserve to be
take back your flow.

you can take back your flow.
 you can stop your flow.

and re-direct it to something new worth your heart and effort.

five big reminders.

you are deeply missed.
you can take all the time you need.
you are in the hearts of many.
your healing process is your process.
your love is irreplaceable.

every month is about you. every second is you.
every season blooms you. and if you didn't know
this)how could you know this(nothing tastes.
nothing feels. nothing sounds. the same when
your star goes missing. when your light fades.
please don't go away. come back. come back.

you don't hear this enough.

you have this power over me)unexplainable power( )don't want to explain it(glad it is your love that is the gravity holding me down. you made my day. everything that happened prior to you isn't worth worrying about. your pour that leaves you is golden honey. every drop of you is filled with gentle sage. you aura your aura your aura is a kind invitation. you are a favorite fragrance so many want to try to bottle. you pour your pour your pour is a beautiful pouring. ghosts that haunt you—tell me about them. you haven't done anything for you in a long time. go do something just for you. someone will take care of what you've been taking care of. you've been away. come back. you've been away. come home. you've been away. come chill. you've been away. come now. showing you love is better than telling you love. telling you love never spoke close to your soul as much as showing you has. becoming fluent in you and your heart language. xo.

allow yourself.

allow yourself to feel.
allow yourself to fail.
allow yourself to fall.
allow yourself to free.
allow yourself to far.
allow yourself to face.
allow yourself to faith.
 allow yourself to flow.
allow yourself to fierce.

allow yourself to grow. to grow without pruning. to grow without trimming. to grow without perfecting. to grow into spaces you were told you shouldn't be in. to grow to be proud of all that has come from you. allow yourself to be who you are with no expectation to change for anyone else.

allowing is a letting. a bestowing. a gifting. a brewing. a sacreding. a trusting. a trusting. a trusting. a risk to bet on the unknown. to breathe in yourself and breathe out doubt. breathe out doubt.

by allowing yourself you admit yourself. you register for all the abundance that is already yours.

allow yourself grace. allow yourself time.
allow yourself mistakes. allow yourself healing.
allow yourself play. allow yourself patience.
allow yourself enough. allow yourself love.

allow yourself to _____.
allow yourself too.

what you deserve to be appreciated for.

everything and your heart.
the behind the scenes love.
just because and in-between.
what you pick up out of your way.
your invisible struggles.
all the changes you've made.
patience for always waiting.
for being a beautiful spirit.
healing what hurts most.
your audacity to bloom.
prioritizing self compassion.
that balance you beam.

***

you deserve more. more flowers. more words. more actions.
more currency that meets you where you are and fills every
bucket of yours that needs filling before you feel empty. before
your feelings go down. before you wonder if you are being
enough. being you shouldn't have to wonder about these things.
but when you close your eyes know that light)that light(is
forever on. it's impossible to unsee a light like you. you are loved
beyond beyond beyond measure. beyond beyond beyond this
place that was never ready for you. the giving. the giving. the
giving. anyone blessed to hold any amount of you in their lungs
knows what it's like not being able to breathe without you.

for when you want to remain neutral.

you can be frustrated.
you can be numb.
you can be confused.
you can be disheartened.
you can be speechless.
you can be cautious.

but you can't be neutral. you can't be idle. you can't be silent. you can't do nothing. not anymore. those days are done. you are for love or you are for hate. there is no gray area. there is no such thing as good on both sides.

after the january 6 riot
in washington d.c. 2021

seven meaningful finds.

finding meaningful love.
finding meaningful work.
finding meaningful friendships.
finding meaningful caregivers.
finding meaningful schools.
finding meaningful guides.
finding meaningful words.

you know when something or someone is right for you.
there is alignment to your core values and there is
grace to push yourself outside your comfort
zone to learn and grow.

eight rehearters.

you are you and that is beautiful enough.
anything done by you is unlike what anyone
else does and that's because you are unique.
worrying about something doesn't make you
a worrier you just like to focus on the details of things.
it's okay to forget special occasions these are strange
and estranged times you can't be expected
to remember the weight of each day.
people will hold grudges against you for things
you weren't aware of or are making amends for.
the light in you is yours. if you believe you can
you will. if you believe you can't you won't.

all that overtime.

all that overtime. all that hearttime. all that.
all that. grinding. pouring. giving. producing.
takes a toll. taking a toll. can be and has been
expensive. but do you see what is happening.
do you feel the yield. of all your all. of all
your work. set aside others applauding or
not applauding. did you applaud. did
you outline all of you and address
your name. frame your goal.
you can't rely on outside highs.
practice clapping for yourself for all
the things no one else will care to clap for.

practice clapping for yourself.

practice clapping for yourself for all the things no one else will care to clap for.
practice clapping for yourself for all the things no one else will care to clap for.
practice clapping for yourself for all the things no one else will care to clap for.
practice clapping for yourself for all the things no one else will care to clap for.
practice clapping for yourself for all the things no one else will care to clap for.
practice clapping for yourself for all the things no one else will care to clap for.
practice clapping for yourself for all the things no one else will care to clap for.
practice clapping for yourself for all the things no one else will care to clap for.
practice clapping for yourself for all the things no one else will care to clap for.
practice clapping for yourself for all the things no one else will care to clap for.
practice clapping for yourself for all the things no one else will care to clap for.
practice clapping for yourself for all the things no one else will care to clap for.
practice clapping for yourself for all the things no one else will care to clap for.
practice clapping for yourself for all the things no one else will care to clap for.
practice clapping for yourself for all the things no one else will care to clap for.
practice clapping for yourself for all the things no one else will care to clap for.
practice clapping for yourself for all the things no one else will care to clap for.
practice clapping for yourself for all the things no one else will care to clap for.
practice clapping for yourself for all the things no one else will care to clap for.
practice clapping for yourself for all the things no one else will care to clap for.
practice clapping for yourself for all the things no one else will care to clap for.
practice clapping for yourself for all the things no one else will care to clap for.
practice clapping for yourself for all the things no one else will care to clap for.
practice clapping for yourself for all the things no one else will care to clap for.
practice clapping for yourself for all the things no one else will care to clap for.
practice clapping for yourself for all the things no one else will care to clap for.
practice clapping for yourself for all the things no one else will care to clap for.
practice clapping for yourself for all the things no one else will care to clap for.
practice clapping for yourself for all the things no one else will care to clap for.
practice clapping for yourself for all the things no one else will care to clap for.
practice clapping for yourself for all the things no one else will care to clap for.
practice clapping for yourself for all the things no one else will care to clap for.
practice clapping for yourself for all the things no one else will care to clap for.

practice clapping for yourself for all the things no one else will care to clap for.
practice clapping for yourself for all the things no one else will care to clap for.
practice clapping for yourself for all the things no one else will care to clap for.
practice clapping for yourself for all the things no one else will care to clap for.
practice clapping for yourself for all the things no one else will care to clap for.
practice clapping for yourself for all the things no one else will care to clap for.
practice clapping for yourself for all the things no one else will care to clap for.
practice clapping for yourself for all the things no one else will care to clap for.
practice clapping for yourself for all the things no one else will care to clap for.
practice clapping for yourself for all the things no one else will care to clap for.
practice clapping for yourself for all the things no one else will care to clap for.
practice clapping for yourself for all the things no one else will care to clap for.
practice clapping for yourself for all the things no one else will care to clap for.
practice clapping for yourself for all the things no one else will care to clap for.
practice clapping for yourself for all the things no one else will care to clap for.
practice clapping for yourself for all the things no one else will care to clap for.
practice clapping for yourself for all the things no one else will care to clap for.
practice clapping for yourself for all the things no one else will care to clap for.
practice clapping for yourself for all the things no one else will care to clap for.
practice clapping for yourself for all the things no one else will care to clap for.
practice clapping for yourself for all the things no one else will care to clap for.
practice clapping for yourself for all the things no one else will care to clap for.
practice clapping for yourself for all the things no one else will care to clap for.
practice clapping for yourself for all the things no one else will care to clap for.
practice clapping for yourself for all the things no one else will care to clap for.
practice clapping for yourself for all the things no one else will care to clap for.
practice clapping for yourself for all the things no one else will care to clap for.
practice clapping for yourself for all the things no one else will care to clap for.
practice clapping for yourself for all the things no one else will care to clap for.
practice clapping for yourself for all the things no one else will care to clap for.
practice clapping for yourself for all the things no one else will care to clap for.
practice clapping for yourself for all the things no one else will care to clap for.
practice clapping for yourself for all the things no one else will care to clap for.

celebrate yourself.

sometimes you have to learn to keep your wins to yourself.
in keeping it to yourself tho make sure you celebrate yourself.

your light is where love is.

the most amazing thing about you isn't always what you think it is or are told it is. it is lingering)lingering lingering(in reach. at hearts reach. the reaching for it. the searching for it. the wanting for it. the digging for it. finding you and then returning you back to the wild. and if there is ever a breaking and entering. a coming in and shattering. a violation. a hurting. may you expand brighter and more beautiful than you were before. you can get through. you can grow through. anything love.

just want to be where you are.
need to be closer to you are.
have to be surrounded by your.
your. your. your. the sweetest
your. whisper in your ear
to tell you the finest lines
of poetry that you are.

your light is where love is. your light is where love is.
your light is where love is. your light is where love is.
your light is where love is. your light is where love is.
your light is where love is. your light is where love is.
your light is where love is. your light is where love is.
your light is where love is. your light is where love is.
your light is where love is. your light is where love is.
your light is where love is. your light is where love is.
your light is where love is. your light is where love is.
your light is where love is. your light is where love is.
your light is where love is. your light is where love is.
your light is where love is. your light is where love is.
your light is where love is. your light is where love is.
your light is where love is. your light is where love is.
your light is where love is. your light is where love is.

four parts of you to envy more.

your heart. rare. big. honorable.
your hands. gentle. caring. giving.
your mind. smart. imaginative. magic.
your kind. thoughtful. loving. attractive.

no one is you but you. don't get caught up in
thinking there isn't a special bone in your body.
every part of you is wonderful. especially those
parts that have gone unwatered gone unnoticed
gone from your admiration. you are noticeable.
remarkable. you can do what no one else can.
be envious of you more. breathe you in more.

fifteen authentic things to say more to each other.

sorry. wish i had the emotional capacity to breathe
with you and show up for you how you need me to.
charge it to my head and not my heart. my bad.
i can see what i did landed on you how i didn't
intend. excuse me. your people sure would be so
proud to see the light you are. what does support
look like. are there parts of you i am failing to water.
i want to water us more. respectfully i disagree and
love you i just don't understand but willing to hear
more learn more listening to embrace not to reprimand.
be who you are. you are becoming. you are beautiful. thank you.

how to prove that you are here.

people feel better around you.
people fill better with you.
people think of your heart.
people breathe deep with you.

proof that you are needed.

people aren't the same without you.
people crave your loving attention.
people look up to your limitless sky.

proof that you are magic. you just proved it.

five ways to live your best life.

know yourself.
love yourself.
accept yourself.
heal yourself.
be yourself.

your path is yours. to pave to traverse to journey.
people will always have something to say about
your life. let them. don't preoccupy your time
and energy to try and satisfy everyone who
isn't you. you know what kind of lights
best guide you. follow your heart.

you already know this.

no one can tell you what to do.
you're doing what you can.
available doesn't mean interested.
can't force what won't fit.
not your responsibility to convince closed hearts.
their ego is trippin not yours.
everyone won't understand you.
boundaries are an act of self love.
you deserve genuine relationships.
someone is always silently cheering for you.
 they can take your style but never your soul.

due for some love.

you did it. you're doing it. if that isn't deserving
of shine and pride and congratulations then you're
due for some kudos. some appreciation. some love.

some of the greatest relationships worth salvaging.

some of the greatest relationships worth salvaging and
remaining in are the ones that propel you and not stress
you. inspire you and not wither you. cherish you and
not damage you. you deserve easy love.

you look good on you.

my goodness you look good on you.
my goodness you look good on you.
my goodness you look good on you.
my goodness you look good on you.
my goodness you look good on you.
my goodness you look good on you.
my goodness you look good on you.
my goodness you look good on you.
my goodness you look good on you.
my goodness you look good on you.
my goodness you look good on you.
my goodness you look good on you.
my goodness you look good on you.
my goodness you look good on you.
my goodness you look good on you.
my goodness you look good on you.
my goodness you look good on you.
my goodness you look good on you.
my goodness you look good on you.
my goodness you look good on you.
my goodness you look good on you.
my goodness you look good on you.
my goodness you look good on you.
my goodness you look good on you.
my goodness you look good on you.
my goodness you look good on you.
my goodness you look good on you.
my goodness you look good on you.
my goodness you look good on you.
my goodness you look good on you.
my goodness you look good on you.
my goodness you look good on you.

six small acts of bravery.

learn.
unlearn.
do something
small. care.
listen. love.

six small acts of bravery
to change the world.

deep you in. deep you out.

deep you in.
deep you out.

the best kind of breath is you love.
the best kind of love is you love.

vulnerability doesn't mean you lose anything.

vulnerability doesn't mean you lose anything.
it means you are giving yourself capacity to gain
giving yourself capacity to love giving others
a heart and a hand and an empathy that has
grace and compassion instead of closing
off instead of pushing back instead of
gaslighting instead it asks and it
wonders and it holds and it
feels and it opens and it
says thank you for
sharing your
truth.

some things.

some things just aren't worth
giving any more energy to.

four types of space you deserve.

safe space. nurturing. nourishing.
brave space. real. truthful. humbling.
open space. inclusive. non-judgmental.
loving space. appreciative. heartful. home.

you deserve the space to space. to define. to break and peace. to piece and unpiece. to prosper. to fragile. to meander. to part and accept. to critical and question. and. and. and. others do as well. everyone has a right to safe. to brave. to open. to loving. spaces. but we need each other. to grow. to learn. to breathe. to fully be human.

you are the greatest enough.

things you hold inside aren't for everyone.
everyone won't see what you see or feel
how you see or feel. the air you turn into gold
because you are an alchemist can't just be
breathed in by those with no understanding
no meaning no intention of keeping you
of staying all the seasons. all the evaporations.
and pourings and deep deep diving. they have
to hold and hold all of you. not pick and choose.
all of you. you aren't one to just let go of. any
breath to come after you will never be enough.
you are the greatest enough. the only enough.

hopes for you.

i hope you face yourself in the mirror and see your self. and when the dark comes and nothing can be seen but shape and outline i hope you fill in the details in ways that inspire you to color in the unknown with your light. your power and your imagination turns shadows into something kind of refreshing. no one else can do that. i hope what you share comes back tenfold. and keeps rolling towards you like clouds on their way home. i hope the rainbow inside you golds and pots and blooms before after and during the waterfall. i hope how you feel gets airtime. gets audience. gets outside. so you can breathe and be. breathe and be. i hope the stress that visits you untethers and you become lighter. i hope you become lighter and fly wherever you want to. i hope that you don't have to justify or rerun your experience every time someone asks. i hope in your quiet you quiet. and find the words you need to tell yourself and water yourself.

how to leave and not feel guilty.

you can't please everyone. some will personally take offense as if you have offended them by doing what you have to do. you cannot control how they react. one day they may understand. one day they will have to do the same. the relationships you have created might look differently but the ones that last are the ones that value growth.

ask yourself: *if i stay*
will i regret staying.

you won't be present if you keep keeping yourself from what is meant for you. what is there to teach you what you need to know. and you won't know if you don't try.

if the fear is failing it's okay to fail. fail fast. fail often. fail and fail and fail. failure is a life lesson. a love lesson. do it more often.

and what if you still feel guilty. about leaving people who you don't want to leave. take them with you. if not physically. spiritually. return when you can. just know they will always be there with you.

how to set a boundary that is long overdue.

i know this was something
you may have thought was
cool was appropriate was
good at the time)i may
have thought so too or
was trying to figure
it out myself(but
no more. no
more.

this no comes with no gray area.
this no comes with no wiggle room.
this no comes with no negotiation.
this no comes with no malice.
this no comes with no explanation.

i may have already told you this
perhaps i wasn't clear clear clear.
but let this be the final clarity
the last statement. this is what
i need. and it hasn't happened
yet. and because of that i'm
going where my needs are
beautifully met. considered.
fulfilled. and overflowing.
it's not for you to understand.
but if you want to then respect
this boundary. respect this space.
respect this choice. respect this
chapter and don't make it
about you.

how to set a boundary that is long overdue. II

don't feel bad if you don't know how to set boundaries. we live in a world where people think everything that isn't theirs is theirs. taught that it's theirs. bodies of others. minds of others. rights of others. they have always been wrong. you are yours. you have always been yours. you are always yours.

for when you are sad.

it's okay to be sad.
no need to rush out of your sadness.
others may try to speed up your
emotions to match their mood
but how you feel is telling
you to be patient with
yourself.

what not to say when someone is sad:

get over it.
don't be sad.
that sucks.
suck it up.
don't cry.
snap out of it.

what to say when someone is sad:

how can i show up for you.
i'm here if and when you need.
how are you feeling.
no need to talk if you don't want to.
what does your heart need to hear.
you are not being dramatic.
there is room for you here.
always room for you here.

beloved. it pains me to know you are in pain. it hurts me to know
you are hurt. i may not grasp the depths of your sadness in your
soul but i will carry it with me. i will keep watch when you eyes
close and your heart cries. days. months. years. forever. forever.
forever. nowhere to go but with you. i am here for you love.

where is your heart.

so many causes. so many battles. so many issues. so many troubles. it can feel overwhelming. it can be too much to process. too much to hold. too much to aware. and yet and yet and yet you are capable to listen. to open. to care. to learn. and that is something worth more than pretending nothing is wrong.

guided questions to ask yourself. to ask others.
about life. when you don't know what to do:

where is your heart.
where is your energy.
where is your mind.
where is your worry.
where is your storm.

how may i serve.
how may i support.
how may i align.
how may i carry.
how may i unload.
how may i accomplice.

we all can do one small thing. it doesn't have to be big. we can be the change. we have to choose the change we want. we can't be idle.

there is no need to struggle alone.

beloved. there is no need to struggle alone
when there is someone willing to hear every word
your soul is aching to say. even if trivial. even if
silly. even if heavy. you don't have to have all
the answers. you just have to be who you are.
never a bother only a blessing. believe that.

you are not a burden.

what do you need to hear. i will tell you.
are you okay. tell me if you are not.
are you hurting. tell me where you're hurting.
what makes your day. i want to make your day.

it's not always what you say it is how you say it.
the caring. the considering. the listening. the loving.
the details of the heart. everyone won't
look in-between or seek what is under but the one
the few the giving will slow and breathe. slow and
notice. slow and witness. you. wonder you. and
you won't feel like a burden. you are not a burden.

care less

if you fail.
if you lose.
if you mistake.
if you are labeled.

care more

if you heart.
if you love.
if you all.
if you try.

you only live once so do this one to the fullest.

the most beautiful hello without saying hello.

you were on my mind.
)you are always on my mind(.
every dream i have is about you.
glad you are here. so glad you are here.
did you feel it too that rumbling that rumbling.
you are more beautiful than i ever imagined.
can this day never end can we stay like this.
i forgot what i was about to say to you.
only person i want to rise with is you.
thank you for meeting me love.
it took us long enough.
you have my heart.

how to be better for your person.

if you can. go sit with your person.
if you can. get on the phone with your person.
if you can. do something for your person.
if you can. better for your person.
if you can. fluent the language of your person.

so often)too often(it is about what can someone
provide what can someone offer instead of what
is it that i can give what is it that i can do what is
it that i can service in service of another in service
of the one the ones the unconditionals who always
bestow so much. they deserve more giving love.

what you should never get tired of hearing.

wow. look at you.
you never cease to amaze me.
not sure how but you get better and better.
always there for you.
i see you. keep doing your thing.
i love you. even if we never speak again.
how can i support you in good times and bad.
let's talk even if there is nothing to say.
you are beautiful.
i want to spend infinity with you.
i'll do anything to protect your heart.
you are my everything. everything. everything.

all the ways in waves you are loved.

you are a fountain. didn't you know. how could you. how could you. natural beauty just pours without wondering if what falls is anything other than raw. so many want to get close to see what's inside you. but there are those)the rare ones like you(who don't worry about your wild because they know. they just know.

the ways and waves of you. tidal.
the ways and waves of you. full.
the ways and waves of you. sage.

there is a reason people retreat to water. retreat to earth. retreat to grand. it covers and recovers. washes and rinses. notices and absorbs. the quiet there. the rush there. the answers there. there is a poem there)that poem(on the edge of your heart. bring it in. and as the tide gets higher don't think about who stays. everything your water touches returns. it's just a matter of you deciding what you want to keep.

all the things you touch grow. as you are sun.
you are seed. you are water. you are soil.
the greatest element that brings life. gives love.
bridges goodness. connects hearts to hearts.

five apologies you truly deserve.

for losing sleep over things that have no business keeping you up.
for caring too much for people whose love will never reach you.
for missing someone you're told you shouldn't miss.
for grieving too long)there is no such thing as grieving too long(.
for following a route less traveled.

***

you are a wild dream.
a wild wild dream.
unheard of. the kind
you don't want to ever
wake from. sometimes
dreams themselves
stop believing in their
reality because some
thing or someone.

i'm sorry for all the sorries that grip your breath. hostage your
heart. stress your body. that you have to keep tight to yourself
for feeling sorry for. for guilt tripping you when you have ever
every every every right not to apologize for. you don't have to
apologize for that heart of yours. for that want or what or how
or crown of yours. you can't keep apologizing for taking space.
making space. creating space that is already yours. your love.
your light. apologize no more.

p.s.
never stop believing
in your own reality.

three things you can control.

spreading love.
giving love.
being love.

the most beautiful kind of person.

you like to do things by yourself. help yourself.
love yourself. figure yourself. define yourself.
will yourself. trailblaze yourself. trial yourself.
and yet you also know when to reach when to
return when to recognize that you need want
require and benefit from the help of another.
you know that asking for a hand is valuable
that asking for a heart is vulnerable that
asking for anything is putting yourself
out there and that can feel scary and
still you reach. return. recognize.
honor in that. honor in you.

for when you start over.

sometimes starting over
is the reset you've been
waiting for.

for when it feels like you're losing.

it can feel like you are losing when you look
around and everyone else is winning
succeeding and leaving
you in the dust. but
you aren't losing. stop comparing your chapter.
you aren't losing. focus on what's in your control.
you aren't losing. anchor back to your why.
you aren't behind. you aren't behind.
you're ahead. closer than you think.
you're ahead. re-define what success means.
you're preparing. for what's meant for you.
trust yourself. trust the process. trust your faith.

how to prove your worth.

you don't have to. you don't have to prove your worth. if they are unconvinced already or treat you less than phenomenal, exhaust zero molecules their way. remember: you are everything you need. and even when you feel average you are amazing. believe in yourself. the power of you. the power in you. rely on the deepest knowing that you are without doubt the greatest wonder to have ever ever ever had beautiful wings and never used them yet.

next time you question yourself answer yourself like you greet the world with each rising and say: *i am more than capable. so i will use this doubt as fuel. take it with me to remind me even when rain falls and splashes it never ceases to be water. and like water. i too am deep and enough.*

hope this reaches you.

you don't have to hold your breath. long exhale after a long day here. drop your frustrations here. wish you would leave that toxic place. that toxic person. that toxic energy. and move into better. you deserve better. nothing to prove here. love is here. come here.

nothing you need to do here.
just be here. here for you.
honored here)you are
honored here(. the
only thing allow
ed here is love
here. all love
here. xo.

how to tell someone you've changed.

your walk. your energy. your air.

share your findings. if you want to.
share your healings. if you want to.
share your wantings. if you want to.
share your nothings. if you want to.

not everyone will be interested
or take interest or have intrigue
for what you bloom into. that's
what change is. you flow to
love and away from anything
not love.

the gradual. the drip. the all at once.
what they see might feel drastic
but your transition has been
a breaking. an entering.
an innering. a work.
that has always
been you.

if they see you. great. if they accept you. great. if they doubt
you. great. if they refuse you. great. change isn't about them.
change is about you. and if they aren't here for you your
change or here for your heart then they're missing out.

tell them: *this is me. this. is. me. for better)i'm so much better(.*
who i was then was for someone else. i was something else.
but this is me. you know me. but this me right here is the one i
choose to be. who i was born to be. i've loved you for you. love
me for me. we can bloom together.

daily reminder.

you've been go go go and less slow slow slow
so slow it down. slow it down. what you have
been working on will be there when you get
back. this is your daily reminder to break.
to pause. to rest. to take care of yourself.

how to talk to someone who doesn't really care.

i will wait until you're done doing whatever it is you are doing. before i continue. that is the only flare you get. that is the only flag i'll throw. i gave you time and attention to speak your peace. to speak your truth. and you don't seem to give the same or any space for me. so with that said i am done vying for your presence. i tried i tried i tried)done trying(. i know what it's like to not be heard. to be silenced. to claw for air. to catch nothing and nothing feels like this. done feeling like this.

done talking. done showing. done teaching. done proving. absence is not meant to get their attention. absence is meant to free yourself from their drought. collect your energy and restore it. gather it. bring it to where they can't quench for it. the water that once was available is now out of stock to them. and if you give them another chance)for they will search for your water your well your wonderful(you can ask what would make this time any different from the last time. and whatever they say will be dry will be arid will be fumed as yours is what they should have paid attention to last season.

how to be a better listener. get off your distraction. say you need time to finish what needs finishing so you can be full present to the sights and sounds of their share. of their pour. of their giving. don't listen to respond. listen to listen. listen to hear all the details. focus and refocus. they deserve your focus.

required words you need to hear.

you are protected. i will protect you.
you are safe. i will keep you safe.
you are loved. i will love you.
you are heard. i will hear you.
you are seen. i will see you.
you are appreciated. i will appreciate you.
you are honored. i will honor you.
you are worthy. i will worthy you.
you are encouraged. i will encourage you.
you are light. i will light you.
you are needed. i will need you.
you are wanted. i will want you.

the greatest thing about you.

the greatest thing about you
is that you can be in a mood
and still have the audacity
to love your person.

what you shouldn't have to always do.

not everyone can turn what they have
into essential abundance. making it more
than enough. fashioning and molding and
creating roses out of concrete. you do this.
but you shouldn't always have to.

for when you just want to be.

everything doesn't have to have meaning
or be of great significance. sometimes just
choosing to be in the moment and going where
your joy is flowing is what you need and
don't have to qualify it or categorize it
or level it to anything other than what
it is. your every day or every second
doesn't have to revolve around
healing or growth or learning.
it can be about being. and
being is good enough.
so be. so be. so be.

habits of a kind soul.

assumes positive intent.
treats you with respect.
asks instead of assumes.
practices the golden rule.
rarely ever interrupts.
first to offer support.

your heart was never meant for anything less.
your love was never meant for anything less.
kindness. sweet kindness. tender expression.
open awareness to appreciate a beauty like you.
unkind souls do not deserve you.

how to build trust.

be consistent. if you can prove you are reliable by being someone that has good habits like being on time. being account- able. being present. then that leaves little room for questioning if you should be someone to turn to. times good or bad you're on speed dial. pick up.

be human. showing and sharing you aren't absent of flaws or free of insecurities. opening your heart instead of closing it off making you hard to read is opposite of what trust is about. model that you are willing to share who you are.

be yourself. if you have to pretend that you have what you don't have or be who you aren't or ever want to be, then when times get serious you can't keep up to be consistent and you'll forget your true self. drop the act. if they don't like you for you they aren't for you. save your energy.

show you care. don't wait until they come to you. ask what they need. ask if there is anything you can do. ask about their heart. not robotic and transactional but truly interested to know if there is room for you to take anything off their shoulder. anything to celebrate. anything to water more of.

follow through. if you say you're going to do something. do it. if you can't do it say you can't do it. don't lead them on for them to think you got it. will get it. will do it. and then turn out it doesn't get done. be honest so expectations aren't in the balance. align your words with actions.

be patient. trust takes time to build. some start off fully trusting and some start off fully not trusting until it is earned. see it like a bank account. if you aren't adding to it and only withdrawing from it then you don't have a solid relationship. do the right things and watch the relationship grow.

do the work. having an attitude of openness and willingness and desire to look at yourself and any blindspots. any behaviors. that cause you to quickly diffuse that and breathe to see more clearly that says you'll look. you'll look. doesn't mean you are perfect. means you're a lover.

status update.

emotionally unavailable.
spiritually healing.

when you need something soul filling.

all the affirmations thrown your way.
all the compliments thrown your way.
all the heard before thrown your way.
you need something with substance.
you deserve something soul filling.

**beautiful isn't how you look.
beautiful is how you feel.**

when you show up show out. play small never.
not for their comfort. nor for their title. not for
their position. the strength of you is how you
treat others. respectfully. eye to eye. love to
love. confidence is not cocky. confidence is
what unlocks doors you think are locked.
to look the part is starter. being the part
is an entirely different story. be who you
are. be what you want to be.
beautiful isn't how you look.
beautiful is how you feel.
take this with you.

when you forget to bring all of your light.

ahead of is holding you. tomorrow is uptighting you.
deadline is stressing you. upcoming meeting sleepless
nighting you. just remember they are people too. the
power you give them isn't real. how you respond to them
is. how you let them stir you is. you are powerful)more
powerful(when you bring all of you with you. when you
show all of your light instead of some of it.

four entitlements.

you are entitled to be inspired by the light of another.
you are entitled to give gratitude for what is yet to come.
you are entitled to change what you give your energy to.
you are entitled to be sad and sit in your sadness.

that human in you)that beautiful beautiful human(
goes through things and faces challenges regularly.
so to expect greatness always or absent blemishes
or having all the right answers or feeling happy
feelings all the time isn't realistic. you are
entitled to experience the entire menu
of you. be you wherever you go.

leave behind what doesn't help you grow.

quickly. release what hasn't aided you swiftly.
from your mind. from your heart. from your any
where near you. keeping it just causes more harm
causes more hurt causes more unnecessary drama
you had no business near in the first place.

what just popped up)whatever that was(may be the very thing
that should be respectfully severed from your vicinity. thinking
about it too much further will result in it continuing to over-
stay. continuing to take advantage of you. continuing to give
nothing to you in return. it must go. it must. go. just because
you detach from something it doesn't mean you are spiteful
or wish bad karma. it just means they or them or whatever it
is can do their thing away from you. the way growth is set up
you have to properly prepare the container. certain particles and
elements and attitudes and energies just aren't conducive for the
best environment. when you figure out what that means you'll
figure out who deserves to be around you and what you will no
longer allow to happen. letting go of what you've held near for
so long can be hard. or it might be really easy. but the feeling will
be the same when you are graced with new roots that didn't have
enough air to bloom. to sprout. to show you more of you. there
is so much beauty in the leaving. there is so much learning in the
leaving. there is so much spacing in the leaving. there is so much
loving in the leaving. leave behind what doesn't help you grow.
and watch you grow more. watch your blocks unblock. watch
your blessings abundant. what your spirit light. this is for your
mental health. this is for your spiritual health. this is for your
occupational health. this is for your emotional health. this is for
your physical health. this is for your social health. this is for you.
and if anyone guilt trips you or shames you for centering wellness.
your wellbeing. they are the ones to stop giving your water to.

if it isn't laced with love it doesn't belong near you.

if it isn't laced with love it doesn't belong near you.
if it isn't laced with love it doesn't belong near you.
if it isn't laced with love it doesn't belong near you.
if it isn't laced with love it doesn't belong near you.
if it isn't laced with love it doesn't belong near you.
if it isn't laced with love it doesn't belong near you.
if it isn't laced with love it doesn't belong near you.
if it isn't laced with love it doesn't belong near you.
if it isn't laced with love it doesn't belong near you.
if it isn't laced with love it doesn't belong near you.
if it isn't laced with love it doesn't belong near you.
if it isn't laced with love it doesn't belong near you.
if it isn't laced with love it doesn't belong near you.
if it isn't laced with love it doesn't belong near you.
if it isn't laced with love it doesn't belong near you.
if it isn't laced with love it doesn't belong near you.
if it isn't laced with love it doesn't belong near you.
if it isn't laced with love it doesn't belong near you.
if it isn't laced with love it doesn't belong near you.
if it isn't laced with love it doesn't belong near you.
if it isn't laced with love it doesn't belong near you.
if it isn't laced with love it doesn't belong near you.
if it isn't laced with love it doesn't belong near you.
if it isn't laced with love it doesn't belong near you.
if it isn't laced with love it doesn't belong near you.
if it isn't laced with love it doesn't belong near you.
if it isn't laced with love it doesn't belong near you.
if it isn't laced with love it doesn't belong near you.
if it isn't laced with love it doesn't belong near you.
if it isn't laced with love it doesn't belong near you.
if it isn't laced with love it doesn't belong near you.
if it isn't laced with love it doesn't belong near you.
if it isn't laced with love it doesn't belong near you.
if it isn't laced with love it doesn't belong near you.

five boxes to always check.

your heart. how are you really doing.
your crew. individual and collective pulse.
your family. what's new and good and needed.
your path. is this where you want to be.
your purpose. are you in your why.

you can't control anything but you & your choices.
so in your choosing make it a good practice to
check in on all that occupies your heart and
mind and spirit. it isn't selfish to evaluate your
circle and your presence in them. if you aren't
being celebrated and loved go elsewhere love.

when you need to face what needs facing.

nothing always goes as it should. plans change.
people change. places change. and if you can
use that good heart of yours to adjust and orient
a way through then that is what it was bound
to be in the first place. it's not about having
all the options all the possibilities all the
strategies it is about having breath to
blow back to the wind. the courage
to find your footing on the edge
on the rocks on the wall the
desire to face what needs
facing.

but you brace for impact. you crash and collide and flame into
beautiful flame and dig for that lesson. remember that lesson.
for the next crash and collide. for the next wall. for the next
edge. for the next rock.

how to open a closed heart.

your heart is closed for a reason.
you don't have to tell me why.
you don't have to re-open wounds
or revisit old chapters to announce
all the reasons you're cautious.
it's okay to be cautious. i am
cautious too. open when you're
ready. or not at all. i'll wait forever
to get a glimpse of your light.

it's no rush. it's no rush. there may be days you're unwilling to be vulnerable with yourself again. if today isn't that day it's okay. it's okay. that part of your story that made the walls go up is a part)not the full(. in the end you'll always be your own hero. you don't need anyone to save you.

to open your own heart you patient with yourself. and you tend to areas that feel tender when you want to. if you want to. listen to intuition that guides you to pull away or get closer to souls that you feel are genuine towards your heart or not. breathe at your own pace. love at your own pace. slowly you.

to open someone's heart you don't pry. you don't push. you don't rush. you don't force. you grace and wait for them to decide if they want to let you in. if you can't respect this you don't respect them and are better off removing yourself from their presence. be a gentle person for them.

how to open a closed heart. II

nothing. dear heart. you can do
nothing. sweet heart. never feel
pressured from me. take all the
time. take no time. your heart
is safe with me. i don't need
to see what's inside to know
how beautiful you already
are. love from you is worth
watching you bravely bloom.

for your journey this week.

no need to be someone else or do what someone else would do. what would you do should be your mantra. taking you with you is all the motivation you need. wherever you plant yourself, that space will be more nutrient. more abundant. more beautiful. that home you call home has been waiting for you to come home.

everyone will want a piece from you. humbly accept that. affirm what feels good and decline what doesn't. you determine where your energy flows and who it flows to.

your heart can handle anything.

your heart can handle anything.
your heart can handle anything.
your heart can handle anything.
your heart can handle anything.
your heart can handle anything.
your heart can handle anything.
your heart can handle anything.
your heart can handle anything.
your heart can handle anything.
your heart can handle anything.
your heart can handle anything.
your heart can handle anything.
your heart can handle anything.
your heart can handle anything.
your heart can handle anything.
your heart can handle anything.
your heart can handle anything.
your heart can handle anything.
your heart can handle anything.
your heart can handle anything.
your heart can handle anything.
your heart can handle anything.
your heart can handle anything.
your heart can handle anything.
your heart can handle anything.
your heart can handle anything.
your heart can handle anything.
your heart can handle anything.
your heart can handle anything.
your heart can handle anything.
your heart can handle anything.
your heart can handle anything.

to see you better.

worry less about being understood.
worry more about whether or not
you're doing what you know deep
down you are called to do. deep
down you are called to be.
erase those old tapes.
erase those old narratives.
that told you untruths.
that told you that you
couldn't. that told you
that you *don't even try*.
that told you *keep out*.
and make a new mirror
a new tape a new narrative
a new recording that reflects
who you truly are.

***

you aren't your mistakes. if someone makes you feel empty they
are the ones empty inside. not you. not you. write down all the
words. write down all the phrases. write down all the things
you need to hear and tell it to you. tell it to you. you don't need
anything or anyone to see you better.

go where your heart is highly celebrated.

your heart is meaningful.
your heart is beautiful.
your heart is sacred.
your heart is _____.

go where you are highly celebrated.
the places you leave will regret
)always regret(they ever
allowed themselves
to overlook
misread
take advantage
of a wonder such
as you.

how to love better.

you have to want to love better. you have to want to love better.

listen. to their body language.
listen. to their heart language.
listen. to their soul language.
listen. to their mind language.

work. on your self.
work. on your past.
work. on your habits.
work. on your wants.

better is a process. the slightest shift can orient you closer or further and can orient you deeper or surface to what it is and who it is you are trying to love better. if you take a breath you'll get clarity on if it is important to: to do. to care. to slow. to find. to unlearn. to work. to listen. to work. to listen. to really love. better.

quicker to: *my bad.*
slower to: defense.

how to do good in the world.

watch the news.
read articles.
listen to stories.
get curious.
fact check.
share insights.
find resources.
wonder why.
have conversations.

it's not enough to go by what you hear from others. or rely only on the words of someone you trust. you have to do your own digging. you have to do your own learning. not because they might be wrong. but because it's your responsibility to understand what's happening instead of being told what to think. what to feel. what to do.

everyone starts where they start. no awards are given for who knew first. there is no hierarchy in that. it is unhelpful to shame those who did not know sooner. but you must want to know. we are all in this. together. might as well find ways to be decent and loving instead of playing who is the real activist.

care for all the beings. as if they were your own. might that be a shifting. might that be a solution. might that be a signal. to stop thinking you shouldn't worry about others. you should. you should.

begin by noticing what is being shared in your feed. at your table. in your community. in your threads. on your phone. notice what is being said. what's not being said. who is saying what. what needs still need to be met. inventory all of this. consider what's missing. something is always missing.

do those you surround yourself with confirm your biases. do you know what your biases are. check your biases.

you change the world by changing yourself.

you do good in the world when you realize your world isn't the only world that exists. just be better to one another. cherish the humanity and the differences and the divine in one another. love isn't the only answer but love is damn sure one of the best cures.

how to love better. II

be accountable. own your stuff.
validate feelings. get out of ego.
analyze patterns. follow the path.
change behavior. rewire actions.

when you know something or someone is not good for you.
good for your health. good for your life. practice moderation.
or let them go.

choose to. change.
choose to. effort.
choose to. respond.
choose to. leave.
choose to. seek.
choose to. therapy.
choose to. talk.
choose to. love.
choose to. better.

better means
wondering about impact instead of closing off.
thinking before you speak.
wanting more information to understand more.
to learn more and to not take it personally.
to listen more. to speak less.
to scan the situation and apologize. and truly
mean it.

reminders to keep your smile for you.

when you feel hesitation and do not want to respond. do not want to engage. and you'd rather do whatever it was you were doing, that's spirit telling you that you're not interested. you're not available. you don't have to respond. you'll be judged no matter what. so be judged while you do what you want to do: what you love. what you feel holds you. no reason to stop your heart from beating because a little rain falls on you. your reign is magic.

the chapter you are writing is evolving. just because you don't believe it doesn't mean that you someone)someone someone(checks for you. you're the first one they look to. the last one they never last. they are your no matter what. silent or loud they know how to color you in when you fade. your someone reminds you smile.

if feeling sad know that sadness is not a bad thing. it's okay to be sad. stay there as long as you need. no need to pretend if you aren't fine. you can still see in the dark.

maybe it wasn't the best day or you think you did bad on something or said something you didn't mean to say and it was taken out of context or nothing seemed to go your way. you are still loved. and true love doesn't expect perfection.

your give. your love. your you. evertimely. ever-appreciated. ever-ever. a holding of breath. a never wanting to release. when with you it's different. a filling different. a dropping of the shoulders and a pace. a sigh. a finally. a finally.

how you know you're blooming.

the growing pains lessen. less tender
where it used to once really hurt.

your pace has picked up when before
you hesitated. doubt doesn't stop you.

what used to preoccupy you
no longer interests you.

what people think of you miss your ears.
what people think of you miss your heart.
what people think of you is the soundless shout.

those that once didn't take you serious
are the same ones taking notice of you.
baffled by you. learning from you.
wanting to be close to you.
your fire has always
been hottest.

it doesn't go away. that feeling. that pit. that emptiness. it just
visits when you slow. when you lift your energy and set it to rest.
but this time the conversation goes differently. you welcome
it. you listen without defense. you wish it well and greet the
next thought. you've been in bloom and just didn't know it.
you've been unfolding and building and adding to your already
thriving self. but this bloom has another element the other
seasons of you didn't. this bloom is a whole new crown. a whole
new whole you. the greatest version yet.

to develop. to step into. to fully grow. everything can't come.
everyone can't come. everyone won't come. bloom in peace.

for when things don't go your way.

this is only temporary.
sometimes you have to feel
the down to work your way
to claw your way to love
your way back to the
heights you haven't
laid your eyes on yet.

keep showing up.
keep pouring out.
keep the why you're
doing what you're
doing front and center.
never forget your why
and you will do
whatever you need
to do to make it work.
to figure it out. to not
stay down but break
through. break
through.

the good in you. the great in you. the grit in you. the pride in
you. maybe this is a set up. maybe this is a test. maybe you have
a chance to try what you've been resistant to. may be. see where
this takes you. when you least expect. when you stop looking.
when you pause: what is meant will happen. will present. will
uncover. will arrive. will rest.

maybe the thinking is to quit. to stop. to move on. to ignore.

but this love in you can't lose. even if it feels like you're losing.

the way out is through. going around doesn't move the mountain. doesn't remove what must be climbed. climb on. climb on.

you are on your way. breathe in.
you are on your way. release.
you are on your way. trust.
you are on your way. believe.
you are on your way. breathe out.

everything will be. okay.
everything will be. okay.
everything will be. okay.

for when they ask you how you do it.

you're doing it again. looking. comparing. judging yourself. thinking you're behind. far behind. no way to catch up. unsure how to get to where they got. clueless how they got to where they are. saying they have everything you want. what you don't know is that they are saying the same. wanting to be you.

being you is the best thing you can ever do.

you carry so much. you are everywhere
all at once it seems. juggling the world
while balancing daily aches and
still smiling. still loving.

when they ask you how you do it you don't know what they mean. you don't know any other choice. you do it because that's you. you how by being you. you *why* by gratitude.

courageous accountability.

accountability is an under taught skill.
easier to run away. courageous to face.

you are significant. you always have been.

there is a sanctity in you. around you. through you. everyone feels it. everyone experiences it. embrace it more. embrace you more. whatever you say someone will be moved. whatever you do someone will be moved. it's not about moving all the mountains. it's about climbing yours. and by summiting and by exploring and by carving your own you inspire others to embark and discover theirs. don't get caught up in changing those who don't want to change. that cannot be your mission. that cannot be your stress. you know what is right and them pushing back isn't your fault. isn't your burden. isn't your task. let them be rocks. you be water. the small things. the incremental things. the hopeful things. the meaningful things. that is part of you. that is your magic. that is your control. you do you so effortlessly. you do you so beautifully. the weight you are carrying. the work on your plate overflowing. the priorities pushed on you. somehow you still fully present. somehow you clock in. somehow you exceed even when you don't feel like exceeding. whoever has your attention whoever has your heart whoever gets your presence better knows what a rock star you are. they better know. they better know. if you are reading this. if you are breathing this. if you are at this line. please know please know please know that you are significant. you always have been. read this again.

what joy looks like.

joy looks like
you: time flies.
feels right.
heart soothed.
peaceful. full.

presence. no matter the chaos.
you arrive and the air shifts.
a flooding)a beautiful flooding(
of you. what lights you. what
freezes fire. nothing else matters.

your reclamation. your choice. your energy. your song. your
medicine.
your sage. your libation. your retreat. your _____.

joy is the opening of a door you've been waiting and yearning
to step through. checking the hour hand. the minute hand. the
ticking. to see if it tocked since the last you checked. the smile
you're smiling. the rest you're resting. the love you're loving.

joy is summer. that summer. when you could be. when you
knew before you knew that that feeling was a feeling you wanted
to feel forever. always. a memory painted on skin. on timeline.
on you.

you. remember you. joy. you. they can't take you. you aren't to be
taken. you're the fine print. the details. the essentials. a must. to
clear. to feel. to balance. to authentic. without you love. without
you joy. everything meaningless. you are too good to not have.

questions to ask and grow deep with your person.

what is the best question anyone has ever asked you?
how is your relationship with you? may i hug you?
how is your heart? how can i support you?
where are you mentally?
are you okay? how is your relationship with you?
how are you...really?
how do you take your coffee?
how can i learn to see all of you?
will you marry me?
are you happy? how can i be a safe space for you?
what keeps you up at night?
what does success mean to you?

empathetic responses.

interesting.
i saw it differently.
curious what i may have missed.
never thought of it that way.
let's circle back to this.
we will figure this out together.

empathetic responses
from the heart. kindness
is a practice we all need.
we all deserve. we all
can extend more.

you didn't fail you learned.

you didn't fail you learned.
there is a difference.

when dealing with burnout.

burnout doesn't allow the best of you to shine. running on fumes will bring you to a complete halt when you no longer have a choice. so make the choice to break and rejuvenate more often before your body and your mind make the decision for you. either way you have to break. so brake. and be deliberate in your breaking. turn off what needs to be turned off. don't check anything that doesn't need checking. give rest a chance to renew your vow to you. to recommit to you. to reconnect to you.

what burnout looks like: energy depletion. losing track of time. disinterest. feeling unappreciated. autopilot. imbalance. pessimism over tasks that used to bring you joy.

ask yourself: *am i happy. am i healthy. am i okay. am i depleted. am i aware. am i open. am i fulfilled. am i rested.*

burnout is real. everyone experiences it. some can spot it quicker. some just pass it off as necessary to earn stripes on the come up to prove to produce to overextend. place boundaries around your mental and emotional and physical wellbeing. so boundary love. boundary.

if your people don't inspire you to rest.
if your people don't inspire you to heal.
if your people don't inspire you to take
care of you. then those people beloved
are not your people.

something always comes.

something always comes. it always does. it may not look or feel
or sound how you pictured it in your heard how you went back
and forth back and forth with hope with hopes with expecta-
tion for it to go your route. your way. your heart already knows
what is coming. sometimes it doesn't have the heart to tell you
until you hear it for yourself. feel it for yourself. that's life. if
everything were to go how we wanted then nothing would last.
we would want more and more and more and more thinking
the more would fill us. more would satiate us. but that is the
beauty. satisfaction comes when you least expect it. take what
is or isn't given and turn it. flip it. convert it. design it and lace it
with love. it will always be better than you found it. for instance:
a goodbye is just a delayed hello on its way back. always on its
way back to you. always on its way back to you. even if going
away. even if gone away. the return is already headed where
your love sprouted.

what may never come: your highest self. if you keep holding
yourself to standards that don't serve you. definitions that box
you. relationships that stifle you. small minds that dim you.
shallow waters that drought you. get to where you're allowed
to vibrate and be vibrant. get there. root there. vine there. and
bring others to grow there with you.

for when you are stressed.

take a breath. i know you hear this a lot. but it will bring you
balance if you feel elevated. if your heart rate is high. breathe.
pay attention to where air is flowing. where you are holding
tension in your body. did you exhale yet. notice anything. notice
your breath more often. do the one thing. the one thing. what-
ever that is. to center you. move. close. water. dance. remove.
something. do something.

when they say don't be sad.
when they say don't worry.
when they say don't think about it.
when they say don't lose sleep.
when they say don't cry.
when they say don't stress.

tell them you are too human
not to water your entire garden.

your heart is clearing.

***

nine signs you are stressed.

short fuse.
quick to anger.
on edge.
difficulty concentrating. restless.
body is tense.
don't want to do anything.
low energy.
unhealthy eating habits.

how to express love.

love is cool. in name. in saying it. but you know what's even cooler. what matters more. is the showing. the practicing. the working. the trying. the expressing. the not letting the performance of love get in the way of the meaning of love. rather you not say it. rather you show it. rather you breathe it. rather you water it. rather you become it.

love is cool. if you're into fire. if you're into energy. if you're into giving. if you're into unfolding. if you're into staying. if you're into letting go and letting in. love is nothing to just play with. love. the best kind of magic. the real kind of magic.

love is cool. protect it.
love is cool. protect it.
love is cool. protect it.
love is cool. protect it.
love is cool. protect it.
love is cool. protect it.

oh love. oh you. the heartbeat.
the lovebeat. if their words and
actions don't fade into your soul
and you can't feel love it ain't love.
it ain't love. love.

five golden rules and nine golden re-definitions.

quiet the noise of others.
listen to your inner voice.
what you consume.
wonder more often.
spread love.

re-define success.
re-define relationships.
re-define happiness.
re-define traditions.
re-define culture.
re-define vulnerability.
re-define enoughness.
re-define belonging.
re-define yourself.

you were never meant to be contained. break free. break
expectations. you were meant to make your own meaning.
your own system to ensure you can thrive. once you let go of
pictures drawn by someone with you not in mind you'll start
creating your own. one where you want things. one where
you define things. one where you include more. more people.
more love. more reverence. more connection. more life. more
authentic belonging. you will bring back goodness. your kind
of good goodness. your all. it's abysmal out here without the
good you bring.

the water in you is magical.

you're ahead but feel behind.
you're avision but feel unclear.
you're afraid but feel _____.

rest assured. rest. assured. it's okay to race yourself. no one to
race but yourself. rest those wild thoughts where you side-by-side
compete with anyone else. rest those wild thoughts where you
always think someone is better than you. bury those thoughts.
start to only pull from your well. water your love there.
well your own love there beloved.

watch what grows.
watch you grow.

the water in you is magical.
the water in you is magical.
the water in you is magical.
the water in you is magical.
the water in you is magical.
the water in you is magical.
the water in you is magical.
the water in you is magical.
the water in you is magical.
the water in you is magical.
the water in you is magical.
the water in you is magical.
the water in you is magical.
the water in you is magical.
the water in you is magical.
the water in you is magical.

you make everything feel better.

you make everything feel better.
you make everything heal better.
you make everything love better.
you make everything taste better.
you make everything want better.
you make everything need better.
you make everything sound better.
you make everything land better.
you make everything hard better.
you make everything sad better.
you make everything better better.
you make everything. better.

it might be because of the tones you use.
or maybe the approach you take. or maybe
there is what can't be named that you do.
whatever it is you are a marvel.

***

even as days get longer and you can't hold on to that smile you
give to others and you need to retreat into a corner and blanket
yourself under what helps you forget your own pain. your own
aches. your own struggles. your own reservations. there is light
)your light(that flutters and pulses and hovers and covers what
is sharp and turns bitter moments into honey. into something
better into better into better into better into better days are
coming. even as days get longer and you can't hold on to that
smile you give to others. hold on to that smile. hold. on.

someone wants to hold you.

someone
wants to
catch you
hold you
like you
hold the
world
softly
gently
lovingly
strongly
lightly.

it's okay to protect your heart.

it's okay to boundary.
it's okay to reinforce.
it's okay to say no.
it's okay to push pause.
it's okay to be alone.
it's okay to want more.
it's okay to keep to yourself.
it's okay to slow.
it's okay to uncertain.
it's okay to change your mind.
it's okay to protect your heart.

notes to breathe in deeply. slowly. lovingly.

you are some body. holy. holy.
you are some soul. special. special.
you are some love. needed. needed.

many would cross all the waters
every single drop of sea and mist
to report back to you. to prove
what doesn't require proving
that you are the wonder that
most wonder about. the dream
that most dream about. the sight
that most sight about. the only
most only about. remember that.

the wonder. the dream. the sight. the only.

you can breathe out now.
breathe out all that you
were holding in.

for when what you deserve to hear never comes.

it may never come.
the words. the acts.
the thoughts.
the courtesy.
the care.
the deserving.
the deserving.
the filling.
the filling.
the feelings.
the appreciation.

you can't expect that person)yep that person(
to figure it out. to recognize you when they
aren't interested in becoming fluent in you.
you can expect after the last warning. the
last plea. the last reminder. that when
you begin to affirm you. when you
begin to breathe you. when you
begin to margin them. when
you begin to release them.
they will drool back.

when it comes up again)it will rise up again(and you need
what may not come. give it to yourself. tell yourself. prayer
yourself. cover yourself. manifest yourself. attract yourself.
affirm yourself. love yourself. love yourself. love yourself. love
yourself. love yourself. frequently. before going empty. you are
never empty love.

i'll tell you. i'll learn you. i'll love you.

it is devastating to know so many yearn for the most simple things. who need the most hearty things. and yet go unseen. go unfulfilled. go on as if they are wrong for needing belonging. needing a love that decodes in their soul. needing what everyone deserves. i'll tell you. i'll learn you. i'll love you.

you already know this. II

that part of you that yearns that aches that always
goes above and anticipates and shows up always
finds reasons to celebrate the little things always
carries the sun on your lips to give light always
sailing for and crewing for common good always
being the first to serve and last to receive always
goes undetected under radar unvalidated and yet
you keep going keep flowing keep moving and
making this place better leaving this place better
as if it was your heart's mission)it is your heart's
mission(to ignite beautiful fires in everyone
everywhere by breathing life. keep breathing life.
outgrowing makes room for ingrowing. your
softness isn't weakness. it's brave. vulnerable.
liberating. it's strong. courageous. inspiring.
your softness is love. anything from you
is momentous. anything from you is
profound. anything from you is
refreshing. anything from
you is ooh.

statements your whole being deserves to hear.

i'm sorry i wasn't there when you needed me there.
you can release every fault that you think was your fault
and forgive yourself for ever thinking you do anything
wrong. you did nothing but love. if anything it was
your love that was needed. give me your sorrows
give me your worries. give me all that you carry.
give me what you keep to yourself. safely i'll
store whatever you have been holding.
when you are away it is hard.
i should have told you
this sooner.

how you know you're blooming. II

thorns become dull. become non-factors.
become lessons. you pull them out instead
of keeping them in and allowing them rule
allowing them access allowing them you.

letter to your last year self.

where you are right now won't always be your story. things are crunchy but you make it out in peace. that person at work getting under your skin is going through a lot. a lot. a lot. they don't have the space to unpack what's going on and work is the only place they feel they have control. charge it to their head and not their heart. what you are keeping to yourself gets a bit heavier because you try to quarter and contain you from you. water that part of you more just by acknowledging that it is there. this will help. the gifts you are gathering now will turn into brighter gems and lessons you laugh about as part of your success story. your healing journey. your transformative glory. stay the course. damn proud that you kept going.

who you used to be. loving.
who you used to be. giving.
who you used to be. kinding.
who you used to be. inclusive.
who you used to be. grateful.
who you used to be. thoughtful.
who you used to be. beautiful.
is still who you are. that will
never change. honor you for that.

you were never strangers but at times it feels like that. even in the same space you grow towards and grow apart. unrecognizable yet familiar. uninterested yet connected. like the game breath plays. like holding air in looking at your person. still. together. you change for you. seems dark now and your energy feels like it's going in places you feel unseen. in places you feel outside. joy is coming in the form of a being you never thought you'd meet. you never thought you'd love. your person is always you.

for when you are having a hard time. IV

i know so much is asked of you.
so much is pulled from you. and
you don't want to take up space.
but you don't need that stress
or worry around me. you can be
strong and mighty and soft and
collapse and still be a warrior.
whatever you need it's yours.
whatever you need i'm yours.

if you or someone you love is experiencing hardship
the best thing you could ever do is to acknowledge it
and talk about it. the worst thing you could do is
deny or dismiss or push it under the rug. find
an outlet beloved. and vent. and vent. and
vent. and vent. venting is healing.

xo. adrian michael

i appreciate you

Adrian Michael Green is a writer, mentor, consultant, speaker, diversity trainer, and educator based in San Francisco. He has published over twenty poetry and prose books that spread messages of positivity, healing, courageous conversations, and love. Adrian Michael is a devoted husband, father, and founder of lovasté, a health and wellness company committed to helping people have better relationships with themselves and others. This compilation serves as another invitation to face yourself and look within—a sacred, beautiful, meaningful, intentional, and challenging daily practice.

adrianmichaelgreen.com
instagram.com/adrianmichaelgreen
lovaste.com
instagram.com/lovaste

THOUGHT CATALOG Books

Thought Catalog Books is a publishing imprint of Thought Catalog, a digital magazine for thoughtful storytelling, and is owned and operated by The Thought & Expression Co. Inc., an independent media group based in the United States of America. Founded in 2010, we are committed to helping people become better communicators and listeners to engender a more exciting, attentive, and imaginative world. The Thought Catalog Books imprint connects Thought Catalog's digital-native roots with our love of traditional book publishing. The books we publish are designed as beloved art pieces. We publish work we love. Pioneering an author-first and holistic approach to book publishing, Thought Catalog Books has created numerous best-selling print books, audiobooks, and eBooks that are being translated in over 30 languages.

ThoughtCatalog.com | **Thoughtful Storytelling**

ShopCatalog.com | **Shop Books + Curated Products**

MORE FROM
THOUGHT CATALOG BOOKS

**THOUGHT
CATALOG**
Books

THOUGHTCATALOG.COM

Printed in Great Britain
by Amazon

40179961R00099